GREATEST WARRIORS
GLADIATORS

ALEX STEWART

W

FRANKLIN WATTS
LONDON • SYDNEY

First published in 2013 by Franklin Watts

Franklin Watts
338 Euston Road
London
NW1 3BH

Franklin Watts Australia
Level 17/207 Kent Street, Sydney, NSW 2000

Produced by Arcturus Publishing Limited,
26/27 Bickels Yard, 151–153 Bermondsey Street, London SE1 3HA

Edited and designed by: Discovery Books Ltd.

Series concept: Joe Harris
Managing editor for Discovery Books: Laura Durman
Editor: Clare Collinson
Picture researcher: Clare Collinson
Designer: Ian Winton

The publisher would like to thank Britannia re-enactment group (www.durolitum.co.uk/) and Deeds of Arms (http://deeds-of-arms.
org.uk/default.aspx) for their assistance in the preparation of this book.
Picture credits:
Alamy: p. 15 (Nick Turner), p. 19 (BlueMoon Stock), pp. 20, 22, 26, 27, 28 (AF archive), p. 23 (The Art Archive), p. 24 (Photos 12);
Arènes de Nîmes – Culturespaces (Marc Fasol): p. 17; Britannia (www.durolitum.co.uk/): p. 4 (Dan and Matt Shadrake), p. 10r (Dan
Shadrake as a Thracian; photograph – petewebb.com), p. 12l (Stephen Knight as a retiarius; photograph – petewebb.com); Corbis:
p. 25 (Michael Nicholson); Deeds of Arms: pp. 10l, 14, 18; Getty Images: p. 16 (AFP); Shutterstock Images: pp. title, 7, 9, 13 (nito),
p. 5 (S.Borisov), p. 6 (Stanislaw Tokarski), p. 8 (Will Iredale), p. 11 (Only Fabrizio), p. 12r (Thorsten Rust), p. 21 (Iakov Kalinin),
Wikimedia Commons: p. 29 (Acquired by William T. Walters, 1883).
Cover images: Arènes de Nîmes – Culturespaces (Marc Fasol): top; Britannia (www.durolitum.co.uk/) (Dan Shadrake as a Thracian;
photograph – petewebb.com): bottom centre; Shutterstock Images (Iakov Kalinin): background.

A CIP catalogue record for this book is available from the British Library.

Dewey Decimal Classification Number: 796.8'09

ISBN: 978 1 4451 1859 8

Franklin Watts is a division of Hachette Children's Books, an Hachette UK company.
www.hachette.co.uk

Printed in China

SL002498EN
Supplier 03, Date 0513, Print Run 2355

CONTENTS

Extreme entertainment 4

Doomed to die 6

Samnite – the stabber 8

Thracian – the slicer 10

Retiarius – the net warrior 12

Fighting women 14

Horsemen 16

Fight school 18

Amphitheatres of blood 20

Horror hunts 22

Gladiators on water 24

Great gladiators 26

Rise and fall 28

Glossary 30

Further information 31

Index 32

EXTREME ENTERTAINMENT

Gladiators were armed **professional** fighters in ancient Roman times. They entertained huge crowds of bloodthirsty spectators with their fighting skills. In deadly battles, they fought for their lives against other gladiators, condemned criminals and wild animals. The more brutal the combat, the more the crowd cheered.

STABBING SWORD
The word 'gladiator' comes from the **Latin** word *gladius*, which means 'sword'. As well as swords, gladiators used other vicious weapons such as spears and knives.

DEADLY ARENA
Gladiatorial fights usually took place in an **arena**, an area covered with sand at the centre of an **amphitheatre**.

COMBAT VENUES

The first gladiator fights took place in public squares, known as forums. From around 50 BCE, as the violent displays grew in popularity, specially designed amphitheatres went up all over the Roman **Empire**.

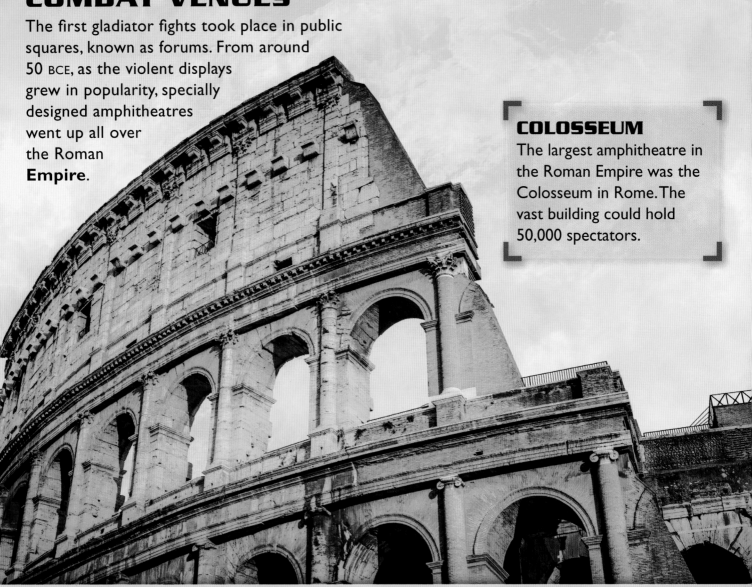

COLOSSEUM

The largest amphitheatre in the Roman Empire was the Colosseum in Rome. The vast building could hold 50,000 spectators.

FIGHTING TALK

First gladiators

Rome got the idea of gladiator fights from the Etruscans and Campanians. These were Italian **tribes** living in regions near Rome. They held bloody 'funeral games' (*munera*) to honour their dead. The first gladiator fight in Rome took place in the city's cattle market, the Forum Boarium, in 264 BCE. Decimus Junius Brutus staged the ruthless show in honour of his dead father. Three pairs of slaves were forced to fight, dressed and armed not as Romans – that would be dishonourable – but as **barbarians** from Thrace. The three losers died.

DOOMED TO DIE

Thousands of gladiators fought and died in arenas throughout the Roman Empire. The majority were slaves, criminals or prisoners of war, who were forced into this fearful occupation. Most gladiators received some training, but few survived more than ten fights.

A DEADLY CHOICE FOR SOME

Some gladiators were volunteers who entered the violent profession out of choice. They were usually ex-soldiers, or very poor people. They chose to give up their freedom in return for regular meals and a chance of fame, glory and prize money in the arena.

DESTINED FOR THE ARENA

As Rome's empire grew, many thousands of prisoners of war were taken. The captives were often forced to fight as gladiators for the Romans' entertainment.

BLOODY BUSINESS

Gladiators could be bought and sold by wealthy Romans, like houses or slaves. A trained and experienced fighter was very expensive – costing perhaps 1,000 *denarii,* which was more than three years' wages for an ordinary Roman. And very occasionally a good (and lucky) gladiator made a fortune. **Emperor** Nero (ruled 54–68 CE) rewarded Spiculus, his favourite gladiator, with a fine house and rich estates.

DEATH ON THE SAND

A gladiator's training included preparation for an honourable death. Gladiators were not expected to ask for mercy or cry out.

COMBAT STATS

A risky profession

- **Risk of death:** Gladiatorial fights did not always end in death. When entering the arena, gladiators faced about a 1 in 4 chance of being killed.

- **Worst chance of survival:** The *andabata* was a gladiator who fought blind. His helmet had no eye-holes and covered his head completely. He was about 99% sure to die.

- **Number of fights:** Very few gladiators had long careers. Flamma, one of the best, had 34 fights, 21 wins, 9 draws and 4 losses.

- **Average age:** Most gladiators died aged between 18 and 25.

- **Longest lived:** One retired gladiator survived to the age of 90.

SAMNITE — THE STABBER

Gladiators were divided into different types, depending on their armour, weapons and fighting styles. Some of the earliest gladiators were known as **Samnites**. They were named after the tough mountain people of Samnium, who were at war with Rome in the 4th century BCE.

SAMNITE
Early Roman gladiators equipped themselves like Samnite warriors.

STABBING SWORD
A Samnite's main weapon was a straight stabbing sword (*gladius*) about 70 cm (27 in) long.

LEG ARMOUR
Metal leg armour known as a **greave** protected a Samnite's lower left leg.

DEFENSIVE SHIELD
A Samnite carried a large rectangular shield, called a *scutum*, to defend himself.

THROAT-DIVIDERS

Advancing behind his large shield, a Samnite tried to close with his opponent and then strike with his stabbing sword. The best target area was the face or neck – a good hit there ended the fight straightaway. That's how the Samnite's sword got its grim nickname, the 'throat-divider'.

CRESTED HELMET

Samnites wore crested metal helmets. These protected their heads, and made them look taller.

ARM PROTECTION

A Samnite protected his sword arm with a guard called a *manica*. The *manica* was a common piece of armour used by many gladiators.

FIGHTING TALK

A gladiator's fate

A fighter could surrender by raising a finger to the referee. His fate was then decided by the umpire or the crowd. Contrary to popular belief, if the crowd gave a gladiator the thumbs down, he was allowed to live. Thumbs up meant sword raised – death!

THRACIAN — THE SLICER

The people of Thrace were famous in the ancient world for being wild and daring fighters. Some of their soldiers had fought with Alexander the Great (356–323 BCE), the amazing Macedonian general whose army was never defeated in battle. The Romans loved having gladiators named after such successful warriors.

CURVED SWORD
Thracians were lightly armed. They wielded curved swords with blades about 34 cm (13 in) long. The swords were short but they were good for slicing opponents.

THRACIAN SHIELD
A Thracian carried a small square or round shield called a *parma*.

THRACIAN HELMET
Most impressive was a Thracian's helmet. The helmet had a wide brim and a visor to cover the face. It was decorated at the top with a mythical bird called a griffin.

GREAVES
A Thracian's leg armour covered the whole of his legs, up to the thigh.

IMPERIAL FAVOURITES

The Thracians were the favourite gladiators of Emperors Caligula (ruled 37–41 CE) and Trajan (ruled 98–117 CE). It is said that when Caligula became emperor he rode across a specially built bridge to his throne – dressed as a Thracian gladiator!

EMPEROR TRAJAN

To celebrate his victory over the Dacians, Emperor Trajan held a festival that included wild animal fights and gladiatorial contests. It is thought that around 5 million spectators came to see the violent displays.

COMBAT STATS

Emperor's celebrations

Following the defeat of the Dacians in the Danube region, Emperor Trajan celebrated back in Italy with 123 days of brutal partying (107 CE).

- **Gladiator fights:** 10,000 gladiators took part in gladiatorial contests as part of the celebrations.

- **Animal deaths:** 11,000 dangerous wild animals, such as lions and bears, were killed during the festival.

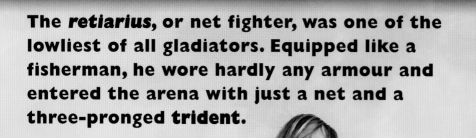

RETIARIUS — THE NET WARRIOR

The *retiarius*, or net fighter, was one of the lowliest of all gladiators. Equipped like a fisherman, he wore hardly any armour and entered the arena with just a net and a three-pronged **trident**.

NET

The *retiarius* relied on a net to entangle his opponent before jabbing him with his trident.

ARM AND SHOULDER GUARD

A *retiarius* wore no helmet, but one arm and shoulder was protected by armour.

THREE-PRONGED TRIDENT

A *retiarius* carried a long, three-pronged spear or trident. He used it to keep his opponent at a distance while trying to trap him in the net.

LIGHT FEET, QUICK ARM

Nimbleness was the key to success as a *retiarius*. Without a shield or helmet, he had to be quick on his feet to stay out of trouble. *Retiarii* usually fought against heavily armed gladiators, such as **secutores** or **murmillos**.

SECUTOR

Secutores, or 'chasers', were specially trained to fight against *retiarii*. They wore helmets as well as arm and leg protection, and they carried a shield and a stabbing sword.

FIGHTING TALK

The fish-man

The *retiarius'* deadliest foe was the *murmillo*, or fish-man. The name came from the fish-style crest on the *murmillo's* helmet. This odd-looking gladiator had an arm guard, leg and feet guards, and a large rectangular shield. His weapon was a stabbing sword. *Murmillo* vs *retiarius* was one of the crowds' favourite fights, with the fish-man often coming out on top.

FIGHTING WOMEN

By the 1st century CE, gladiatorial contests had become lavish, weird and horrible. They featured wild animals, dwarves, children and women. Throwing females into the arena was seen as something special.

NOVELTY ACTS

In Roman eyes, fights between females made an unusual change from contests between male gladiators. Women were made to battle with wild animals or put on armour and hack at each other like male gladiators.

TWO-AGAINST-ONE
Women gladiators usually fought each other, not men. Sometimes they had to fight in two-against-one contests like this one.

WOMEN WARRIORS

Like male fighters, most female gladiators were slaves or prisoners of war. Scholars believe that they were trained to fight, but not in the all-male gladiator schools. They usually fought with swords and shields, and wore arm protectors and greaves on the lower leg. They were rarely given the protection of a helmet.

BATTLE REPORT

Imperial nasties

The cruellest shows seem to have been organized by the emperors themselves. In 66 CE Nero organized a massive battle between two groups of men, women and children. Twenty three years later, in the time of Emperor Domitian, a battle was arranged between an army of women and an army of dwarves. We do not know who won.

HORSEMEN

Gladiatorial contests mirrored combat on the battlefield. Just as armies had **cavalries**, there were mounted gladiators who fought on horseback. These horsemen, or *equites*, were the cream of the gladiators.

A FAIR FIGHT
To make for an even fight, *equites* only fought each other. The battles began on horseback but usually ended on foot.

SHIELD
Equites carried shields about 46 cm (18 in) in diameter.

BATTLE HORSE
In Roman times, a good horse cost as much as a new family car costs today. They were ridden without **stirrups**, which had not been invented.

ENTER THE BRITS

After conquering Gaul (France), in 55 and 54 BCE Julius Caesar came to
Britain. Here his soldiers found a new weapon, the war chariot. Before long,
gladiators (known as *essedarii*) were fighting each other from chariots back
in Rome. Because horses and chariots were costly, these thrilling gladiatorial
contests were the most expensive of all.

FIGHTING TALK

Deadly chariots

There are reports of some of Rome's enemies using 'scythed chariots' – chariots
with knives sticking out of the axels on either side. We do not know for sure
whether scythed chariots were used in the gladiatorial arena – but if so, they
would certainly have made the shows more gory!

FIGHT SCHOOL

Gladiators were professional fighters who were expected to put on a good show. To guarantee this, from 105 BCE, they trained in special gladiator boarding schools. Here, a gladiator learned to fight with skill – and to die bravely.

WEAPONS TRAINING
Gladiators were given training in different fighting styles and techniques. Students practised with wooden or blunted weapons.

TOUGH TRAINING

At school, most gladiators lived and slept under guard so they could not escape. They were fed a special high-energy vegetarian diet of cereals and dried fruit, and given top-level medical attention, including regular massage. Each group of gladiators (*familia*) was trained by a manager (*lanista*) who could hire them out for a good price.

READY FOR THE ARENA
No owner wanted to lose one of his valuable gladiators. Trainees were ready to enter the arena only when they had proven themselves skilful enough to reach the top grade (*primus*).

FIGHTING TALK

A gladiator's oath
On becoming a gladiator, a recruit swore this oath: 'I promise to endure to be burned, to be bound, to be beaten, and to be killed by the sword.'

AMPHITHEATRES OF BLOOD

The earliest Roman amphitheatre was built of wood in about 110 BCE. Larger stone amphitheatres followed and eventually there were amphitheatres in some 230 important towns and cities all over the Roman Empire.

BLOOD AND SAND

Amphitheatres were usually oval in shape. They had tiered seating so every spectator had a good view. At the centre was the arena, a word that comes from the Latin *harena*, meaning fine sand. The sand on the floor of amphitheatres helped to soak up the blood. On games days, pine cones were burned in special holders around the arena. The strong, sweet smell hid the stench of blood and gore.

ANCIENT SITE OF SLAUGHTER

The Colosseum in Rome, shown below, is now partly in ruins, but it remains an impressive symbol of Roman imperial power. For hundreds of years, this immense building served as the venue for Rome's spectacular gladiatorial contests, and it was here that many thousands of gladiators and animals met their deaths.

ANCIENT ARENA
The original flooring of the Colosseum, which has now collapsed, was laid over the stone and brick passages running underneath it.

COMBAT STATS

The Colosseum

- **Date of construction:** begun 72 CE, finished 80 CE
- **Opening celebrations:** 100 days of gladiator fights
- **Maximum capacity:** 50,000 spectators
- **Wild animals slaughtered:** 9,000 in the 100-day opening celebrations alone
- **Most gladiators in one event:** 10,000 in 123 days of contests = 81 gladiators per day for half a year
- **Total number of people to die in the Colosseum:** 500,000 (estimated)

HORROR HUNTS

By the time of the first emperor, Augustus (ruled 27 BCE–14 CE), gladiatorial displays usually included mock animal hunts. Wild beasts were brought to Rome from Africa, Asia and Europe. The animals were slaughtered as a gory warm-up before the main event.

BEASTS FOR SLAUGHTER

Exotic creatures were particularly popular with audiences. The animals killed in Roman arenas included bears, snakes, panthers, giraffes, crocodiles and elephants.

TIGER ATTACK
A fully grown tiger was more than a match for an armed man.

CONDEMNED TO THE BEASTS

Fully trained gladiators were rarely asked to fight animals. The usual beast-fighters (*bestiarii*) were untrained criminals or prisoners. From around 100 BCE, a common death penalty was *damnatio ad bestias* – condemned to the beasts. Instead of being hanged or crucified, the guilty person was thrown into an arena to be torn to pieces – normally by lions.

BEAST VS GLADIATOR

A Roman mosaic from the 4th century CE depicts a gladiator fighting a wild beast.

COMBAT STATS

Order of play at a gladiatorial display

- **Six weeks in advance:** publicity leaflets and posters
- **Nightfall (7 pm) on day before the contest:** feast for gladiators
- **Sunrise (5 am) on day of contest:** detailed programmes (*libelli*) available
- **Early morning (9-10 am):** procession (*pompa*) into arena
- **Mid morning (11 am):** wild beast hunt
- **Late morning (12 noon):** executions
- **Early afternoon (2 pm):** comedy shows, including mock fights
- **Afternoon (3-6 pm):** gladiatorial fights
- **Evening (7 pm onwards):** female gladiatorial contests
- **Night (around 9 pm):** closing ceremony, music and clearing up begins

GLADIATORS ON WATER

In 46 BCE, the brilliant Roman general Julius Caesar introduced a new kind of gladiatorial contest. This was the mock naval battle or *naumachia*. The show involved real ships, packed with gladiators, fighting each other on a lake or in a specially flooded arena.

BATTLESHIP

Roman warships were powered by sails and, in battle, rows of oars. A **trireme** had about 170 rowers and 60 soldiers on board. The aim was to **ram** an enemy vessel and sink it.

NAUMACHIA

In 42 BCE, Emperor Augustus built this special amphitheatre on the right bank of the River Tiber for naval battles. It was approximately 533 x 355 m (580 x 390 yd) and had room for 30 warships with 3,000 fighting men on board.

COMBAT STATS

- **Largest recorded** *naumachia*: staged in 52 CE, by Emperor Claudius (ruled 41-54 CE), on Lake Fucino
- **Number of ships:** 24 full-size triremes (three banks of oars) and 26 **biremes** (two banks of oars)
- **Opposing fleets:** Rhodians (from Rhodes) vs Sicilians, with 2 fleets of 25 ships each
- **Number on board:** 1,900 sailors and warriors, all criminals due to die, with each side commanded by one retired gladiator
- **Size of crowd:** 500,000
- **Battle salute:** before the battle, the competitors said to the emperor '*Morituri te salutant*' - 'Those about to die salute you!'

GREAT GLADIATORS

For some brave and skilful gladiators, success in the arena brought wealth, fame and glory. For a few, it even brought freedom. Great gladiators were as famous in Rome as sports stars are today.

SPARTACUS

Spartacus, played here by Andy Whitfield in the television series *Spartacus: Blood and Sand* (2010), was one of the most famous gladiators of all. His story has inspired people ever since to fight against slavery, cruelty and injustice.

FIGHTING TALK

The greatest gladiator

The Greek soldier Spartacus was sent to a gladiator school. In 73 BCE, he broke out and formed a rebel army of slaves and gladiators to fight against the Romans. Camped on Italy's Mount Vesuvius, they defeated several Roman forces sent against them. Eventually, in 71 BCE, they were defeated in the Battle of Sele. Spartacus' body was never found. 6,000 of his followers were crucified.

REWARDS FOR SUCCESS

As well as prize money, a victorious gladiator would be given a crown or palm branch. If he had impressed the spectators with his skill and courage, they would sometimes throw down money for him. After a famous fight that ended in a draw in 80 CE, Emperor Titus gave both the gladiators – Priscus and Verus – their freedom.

HITS WITH THE GIRLS

Roman writers tell us that muscular gladiators were very popular with the women in the audience. The better-looking gladiators were never short of a date, although they had to keep the meetings secret.

CELEBRITY STATUS

Victorious gladiators often had huge numbers of fans, just like the actor Russell Crowe, seen here in the film *Gladiator* (2000).

At the height of their popularity in the 1st century CE, gladiatorial shows were costing around 180,000 *denarii* to put on – that's at least £250,000 in today's money. By the 4th century CE, the Roman Empire was poorer. Attitudes were changing, too, and the games gradually died out.

GLADIATOR COMMODUS

Emperor Commodus (ruled 161–192 CE), played here by Joaquin Phoenix in the film *Gladiator* (2000), was famous for entering the arena himself dressed as a gladiator. He butchered numerous animals, including elephants and giraffes.

SPIRALLING COSTS

The first gladiatorial contests were organized by wealthy individuals. As the displays became more lavish, costs rose and they were largely taken over by the emperors. The shows became part of the government's entertainment programme of public games or *ludi*. They were popular with many Roman emperors, who saw them as a way of winning approval and displaying their wealth and power.

CHRISTIANS IN THE ARENA

By around 100 CE, the Christian religion was spreading across the Roman Empire. Christians, who said gladiatorial fights were murder, were thrown to the lions for refusing to worship the emperor.

AN END TO CRUELTY

Many emperors, starting with Constantine in 325 CE, ordered gladiatorial shows to stop. Their commands were not always obeyed. In 365 CE, Christians were still being thrown to the lions for having an illegal faith. However, after Emperor Theodosius made Christianity the official religion of the empire, gladiatorial games gradually came to a stop.

CONDEMNED TO THE LIONS

A painting by Jean-Leon Gérôme (1883) depicts a group of Christian prisoners who have been condemned to face the lions.

FIGHTING TALK

Emperors in the arena

At least eight Roman emperors – Caligula, Caracalla, Commodus, Didius Julianus, Geta, Hadrian, Lucius Verus and Titus – are said to have fought as gladiators. In fact, they all fought 'staged' fights and never put themselves in real danger. Commodus, who called himself a *secutor*, shot 100 lions from a safe platform and cut the heads off ostriches.

GLOSSARY

Amphitheatre (Meaning 'place for all-round viewing'.) A circular or oval stadium with an arena in the centre.

Arena A sand-covered circular or oval space at the centre of an amphitheatre where gladiators fought.

Barbarian The Roman word for non-Romans (literally 'bearded ones').

Bireme A warship with a sail and two banks of oars on each side.

Cavalry Warriors who fought on horseback.

Denarius A Roman coin (plural *denarii*).

Emperor The head of an empire.

Empire A country or state and all the lands it controls.

Equites The Latin word for cavalry and for gladiators who fought on horseback.

Greave Leg armour.

Latin The language of the Romans.

Murmillo A gladiator with a fish-style crest on his helmet.

Professional Working or fighting as one's job, for pay or other rewards.

Ram To use a large metal spike to smash an enemy ship.

Retiarius A gladiator who fought with a net and trident.

Samnite Someone from Samnium in central Italy; also an early type of gladiator.

Secutor A type of gladiator that was trained to fight a *retiarius*.

Stirrup One of two metal hoops for a horse rider's feet, helping them balance.

Thracian Someone from the region of Thrace; also a type of gladiator.

Tribe A large group of people living together, like a clan.

Trident A lance with three prongs at the end.

Trireme A warship with a sail and three banks of oars on each side.

Books

Guillain, Charlotte. *Gladiators and Roman Soldiers*. Raintree, 2011.

Burgan, Michael. *Life as a Gladiator*. Capstone, 2010.

Watkins, Richard Ross. *Gladiator*. Houghton Mifflin, 2001.

Malam, John. *You Wouldn't Want to Be a Roman Gladiator!* Franklin Watts, 2012.

Websites

Beware – there are many unreliable sites on gladiators.

BBC History: Romans
www.bbc.co.uk/history/ancient/romans/
The best site for young people, from the BBC – historically accurate, with a good piece on the Colosseum. There's a fun game, too!

Roman Gladiators
www.historyforkids.org/learn/romans/games/circus.htm
A simple but child-friendly site. Not a great deal of specific information but a useful reading list at the end.

Gladiator
http://en.wikipedia.org/wiki/Gladiator
This Wikipedia entry is historically accurate and, although written for adults, the language is not too difficult. There are links to dozens of related subjects, such as Samnites.

Gladiators of Ancient Rome
http://legvi.tripod.com/gladiators/id1.html
Another site written with adults in mind – fine for teachers preparing class material of their own. It doesn't contain much that is not in Wikipedia, but the layout is clearer. The sections on topics such as weapons and common misconceptions are most useful.

Index

amphitheatres 4, 5, 20–21
andabata 7
animals 4, 11, 14, 21, 22, 23, 28, 29
arenas 4, 11, 17, 19, 20, 23, 24, 26, 28
armour 9, 14, 15
  murmillo 13
  retiarius 12
  Samnite 8, 9
  secutor 13
  Thracian 10
Augustus, Emperor 22, 25

bestiarii 23

Caesar, Julius 17, 24
Caligula, Emperor 11, 29
chariots 17
Christians 29
Claudius, Emperor 25
Colosseum 5, 21
Commodus, Emperor 28, 29
Constantine, Emperor 29
criminals 4, 6, 23, 25

deaths 7, 11, 18, 21, 22

emperors 7, 11, 15, 22, 25, 27, 28, 29
  as gladiators 28, 29

equites 16–17
essedarii 17

female gladiators 14–15
fish-man 13
Flamma 7
funeral games 5

helmets 7, 12, 15
  murmillo 13
  Samnite 9
  secutor 13
  Thracian 10
horses 16–17

lions 23, 29

murmillos 13

naumachia 24–25
naval battles 24–25
Nero, Emperor 7, 15
net fighter 12–13

oath, gladiator's 19

prisoners 6, 15
prize money 6, 27

retiarius 12–13
Roman Empire 5, 20, 21, 28, 29

Rome 5, 8, 17, 21, 22, 26

Samnites 8–9
schools 15, 18–19, 26
secutores 13, 29
shields 13, 15
  equites 16
  murmillo 13
  Samnite 8, 9
  Thracian 10
slaves 6, 7, 15, 26
Spartacus 26
spectators 4, 5, 11, 20, 21, 27
Spiculus 7
sword 4, 13, 15, 19
  Samnite 8, 9
  Thracian 10

Thracians 5, 10–11
training 7, 13, 15, 18–19
Trajan, Emperor 11
trident 12

weapons 4, 15, 18
  murmillo 13
  retiarius 12
  Samnite 8, 9
  secutor 13
  Thracian 10
women 14–15

GREATEST WARRIORS

SERIES CONTENTS

GLADIATORS • Extreme entertainment • Doomed to die • Samnite – the stabber • Thracian – the slicer • *Retiarius* – the net warrior • Fighting women • Horsemen • Fight school • Amphitheatres of blood • Horror hunts • Gladiators on water • Great gladiators • Rise and fall

GREEK SOLDIERS • Greece at war • Warrior kings • All-powerful hoplites • Hoplite training • Battle armour • Weapons of war • The mighty phalanx • Warships • Citadels and sieges • Wars with Persia • Persian defeat • Alexander the Great • Greece vs Rome

KNIGHTS • Mounted warriors • Shining armour • Weapons of war • The medieval battle horse • Training a knight • Tournaments • Invasion forces • Battle • Castle strongholds • Prisoners and hostages • Civilized knights • Mythical knight: King Arthur • A new era

PIRATES • Robbers of the sea • Pirates of the Golden Age • Bloody buccaneers • Tricks and terror • Blackbeard • Armed to the teeth • Ship ahoy! • Take aim ... fire! • Attack! • Stolen treasure • Pirate women • The pirate knight • Pirates of the China Seas

ROMAN SOLDIERS • Imperial army • Crack troops • Officers in command • Equipped for conquest • Dressed for war • Back-up troops • Fighting as a unit • Firepower • Making camp • Forts and frontiers • The sacred eagle • The greatest commander • End of empire

VIKINGS • Viking raiders! • Battle ready • Weapons of war • Battle armour • Close combat • Sailing to war • Raids and plunder • Grand armies • Pitched battle • Berserk! • Warriors on the defence • Warriors of the world • Viking twilight

TEN THOUSAND POISONOUS PLANTS IN THE WORLD

PAUL ROCKETT

W
FRANKLIN WATTS
LONDON•SYDNEY

First published in 2014 by Franklin Watts

Franklin Watts
338 Euston Road
London NW1 3BH

Franklin Watts Australia
Level 17/207 Kent Street
Sydney, NSW 2000

Editor: Rachel Cooke
Design and illustration: Mark Ruffle
www.rufflebrothers.com

Dewey number: 581.6'59
HB ISBN: 978 1 4451 2674 6
Library ebook: 978 1 4451 2680 7

Printed in China

Franklin Watts is a division of Hachette
Children's Books, an Hachette UK
company.
www.hachette.co.uk

*Every attempt has been made to clear copyright.
Should there be any inadvertant omission please
apply to the publisher for rectification.*

Picture credits: AVTG/istockphoto: 21c; Peter
Barritt/Alamy: 23br; Charles Brutlag/Shutterstock:
15tc; Chevanon/Shutterstock: 21t; Ethan Daniels/
Shutterstock: 23bl; digital94086/istockphoto: 29b;
Dimijana/Shutterstock: 10c; Edith Dorsey Raff/Alamy:
11t; Dr John Dransfield/RBG Kew: 9b; EcoPrint/
Shutterstock: 23cr; Mark Goddard/istockphoto:
11b; Volodymyr Goinyk/Shutterstock: 22b; Chris
Hill/Shutterstock: 15tr; Ioflo69/istockphoto: 29c;
Juniors Bildarchiv Gmbh/Alamy: 23tr; kanusommer/
Shutterstock: 29t; Tamara Kulikova/Shutterstock:
24b. Majeczka/Shutterstock: front cover bc. Andrew
McRobb/RBG Kew: 9t; Mexrix/Shutterstock:front cover
tr; Jeng Niamwhan/Shutterstock: 15tl; Dr Moreley
Read/Shutterstock: 4b, 23cl; Peter Ryan: 9ca; Sanevich/
Shutterstock: 28; Sursad/Shutterstock: 25t; Saru T/
Shutterstock: 9c. Jordan Tan/Shutterstock: front cover
c; Timobaggibs/Shutterstock: 17t; Natalie Spelier
Ufermann/Shutterstock: 20c; Zhuda/Shutterstock: 27t.

*Throughout the book you are given data relating
to various pieces of information covering the topic.
The numbers will most likely be an estimation based
on research made over a period of time and in a
particular area. Some other research may reach
a different set of data, and all these figures may
change with time as new research and information is
gathered. The numbers provided within this book are
believed to be correct at the time of printing and have
been sourced from the following sites:*
algaeindustrymagazine.com; antarctica.ac.uk;
aquaphoenix.com; bbc.co.uk; bbka.org.uk;
belladonnakillz.com; bio.umass.edu; biologie.uni-
hamburg.de; botany.org; britannica.com; caes.uga.edu;
chemistry.about.com; conifersaroundtheworld.com;
conservatree.org; cultivatorscorner.com; currentresults.
com; cuyabenolodge.com; desertusa.com; dhs.
wisconsin.gov; education.nationalgeographic.co.uk;
encyclopedia2.thefreedictionary.com; eoearth.org;
equalexchange.coop; fairtrade.org.uk; gardenorganic.
org.uk; goarticles.com; guinnessworldrecords.com;
imnh.isu.edu; iucn.org; iucnredlist.org; kew.org;
kids.britannica.com; livingrainforest.org; metoffice.
gov.uk; microscopy-uk.org.uk; naturalfibres2009.
org; nature.com; news.discovery.com; news.
nationalgeographic.co.uk; nhm.ac.uk; oxtreegen.
com; princeton.edu; rainforestconcern.org; rfs.org.
uk; sciencedaily.com; scienceforkids.kidipede.com;
statisticbrain.com; svalbardflora.net; telegraph.
co.uk; topnotchtreeservicestjoemo.com; thompson-
morgan.com; tropicaltraditions.com; vcbio.science.
ru.nl; woodlands.co.uk; woodlandtrust.org.uk;
worldanimalfoundation.net.

CONTENTS

COUNTING DOWN THE PLANT KINGDOM   4

THERE ARE 321,212 SPECIES OF PLANT   6

60,242 PLANTS ESTIMATED AT RISK OF EXTINCTION   8

THERE ARE TEN THOUSAND POISONOUS PLANTS IN THE WORLD   10

OXYGEN IS RENEWED BY PLANTS EVERY TWO THOUSAND YEARS   12

A POMEGRANATE CAN HAVE AS MANY AS 1,370 SEEDS   14

IT CAN TAKE 312 WEEKS FROM SEED TO APPLE   16

THERE ARE MORE THAN 300 TYPES OF HONEY   18

THE TALLEST TREE IS 115.54 METRES HIGH   20

100 SPECIES OF MOSS GROW IN THE ANTARCTIC   22

80-85 COCOA BEANS IN AN AVERAGE CHOCOLATE BAR   24

IT TAKES 14 TREES TO MAKE ONE TONNE OF

MAGAZINE PAPER   26

THE QUEEN OF THE NIGHT BLOOMS FOR

ONE NIGHT EVERY YEAR   28

FURTHER INFORMATION AND LARGE NUMBERS   30

GLOSSARY   31

INDEX   32

Plants can be found all over the world.

They are living organisms that, unlike animals, cannot move by themselves.

PLANTS WERE THE FIRST LIVING ORGANISMS ON EARTH

More than **2,000,000,000 years ago**, a form of algae started life underwater. Around **473,000,000 years ago** liverworts started growing on land. These evolved into many different plant forms. The last form, flowering plants, appeared **140,000,000 years ago**.

Plants produce their own food. They absorb energy from the Sun, which along with carbon dioxide and water, enable them to make food and oxygen. This process is called photosynthesis.

Conifers
290,000,000 years ago

Flowering plants
140,000,000 years ago

Algae
2,000,000,000 years ago

Ferns
360,000,000 years ago

Mosses
470,000,000 years ago

Liverworts
473,000,000 years ago

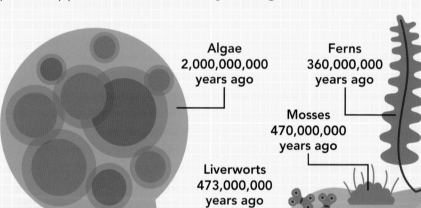

Plants provide the world with oxygen, which is key to the survival of all animals. From plants, we also get food, wood and medicines.

IF THERE WERE NO PLANTS YOU WOULDN'T BE ABLE TO LIVE.

O_2

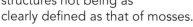

Liverworts are often put into the same plant group as mosses. However there are differences, including their leaf and root structures not being as clearly defined as that of mosses.

BOTANY

Botany is the scientific study of plants. A botanist is a plant explorer, who studies plant structures and how they grow. They may do this in a science lab, or outside in the plant's environment, such as the rainforest or garden.

Numbers play an important role in botany. They are used for calculating statistics and looking for patterns within cell structures and rates of growth.

COUNTING THE RINGS OF A TREE

You can work out the age of a fallen tree by counting the rings on its stump. Each ring represents one year of growth. A large distance between each ring tells us that it was a wet and rainy year. A small distance between the rings tells us it was a hot year.

This tree was 14 years old.
- First year growth
- Rainy year
- Dry year
- Scar from forest fire
- 14th year of growth
- Bark

COUNTING PLANTS WITHIN A FIELD

If you wanted to get an estimate of the kind of plant life and the amount of plant life that grows in a nearby field, get hold of a metre square and throw it into the field. Wherever it lands, count and record the plants that you find.

A FIELD

A metre square is a good size – it shouldn't take too long to count all of the life that you capture within it.

You can then multiply this amount by the size of the field. This will give you an estimate of the number of plants and plant species within the entire field.

Plants grow all around us, in gardens and parks, but also in less accessible places, such as rainforests, deserts and at the bottom of the ocean.

The large number of plant species all over the world makes the task of counting and identifying each one impossible. However, many people attempt to do this, with differing results. The number of plant species identified varies from **300,000** to **380,000**.

The World Conservation Unit estimates the number of plant species as being **321,212**. They have divided plant life into five categories: flowering, conifers, ferns, mosses and liverworts and red and green algae.

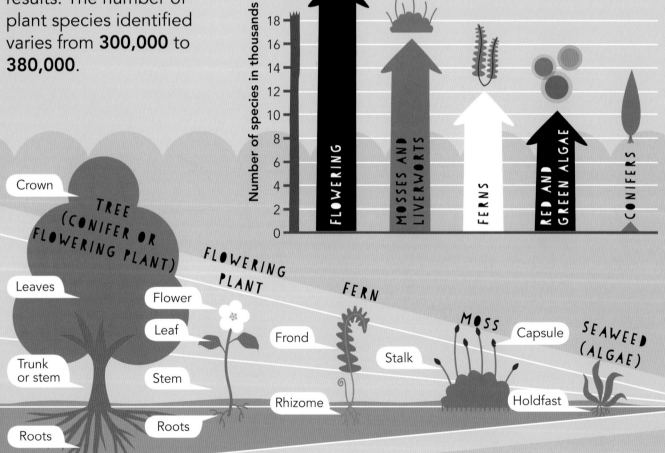

PARTS OF A PLANT
Most plants have roots, leaves and stems. Plants may have parts that differ from each other, but they all have elements that help them perform similar functions. For example, the frond of the fern is similar to the leaf of a tree, the capsule on moss is similar to a flower.

ROOTS

Roots keep plantsfirmly connected to the ground. In flowering and coniferous plants there are two main kinds of roots:

Fibrous roots • • • • • • • •
These are spread out in many directions and all tend to be the same size.

• • **Tap roots**
This is one large root with smaller roots coming off it. Root vegetables, such as carrots and parsnips, are tap roots.

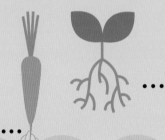

Saint Benedict
A Catholic Voluntary Academy
Duffield Road, Darley Abbey
Derby
DE22 1JD

IDENTIFYING PLANTS

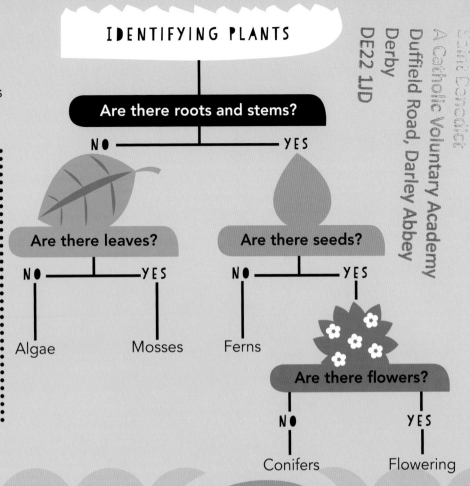

Are there roots and stems?

NO ——————— YES

Are there leaves?

NO ————— YES

Algae — Mosses

Are there seeds?

NO ————— YES

Ferns

Are there flowers?

NO ————— YES

Conifers — Flowering

ALGAE

Not all scientists include algae as a type of plant. Algae do not always appear with a root-like structure, with some, like the microscopic diatom, existing as just a single, individual cell.

DIATOM

Algae are largely found in areas of water, on the surface or bottom of lakes, rivers and oceans. Some types of seaweed and kelp are forms of algae. Many scientists believe that the blue-green algae were the first living things to appear on planet Earth.

SEAWEED

FUNGI

Fungi are organisms that includes mushrooms, yeasts and moulds. They used to be part of the plant kingdom, but since 1969 they have been separated into their own kingdom. They may look like plants, but they have a different cell structure and don't produce their own food. In fact, many scientists believe that fungi are more closely related to animals than to plants.

60,242 PLANTS ESTIMATED AT RISK OF EXTINCTION

Some scientists have estimated that one in five species of plant is at risk of dying out. If there are 321,212 species of plant, that's 60,242 plants at risk.

THREATS TO PLANT LIFE

The main threat to plant life is caused by humans, largely through the clearance of natural habitats for agriculture and industrial development.

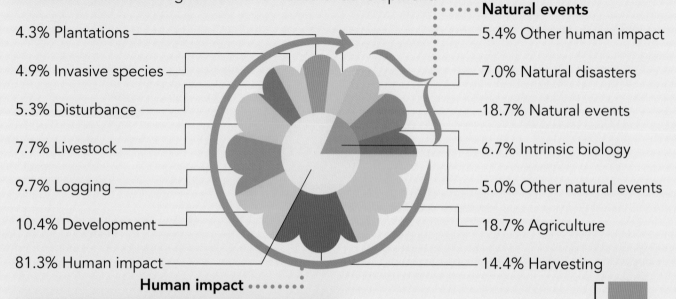

4.3% Plantations

4.9% Invasive species

5.3% Disturbance

7.7% Livestock

9.7% Logging

10.4% Development

81.3% Human impact

Human impact

Natural events

5.4% Other human impact

7.0% Natural disasters

18.7% Natural events

6.7% Intrinsic biology

5.0% Other natural events

18.7% Agriculture

14.4% Harvesting

FROM VULNERABLE TO EXTINCT

The large number of plant species makes it very difficult for botanists to assess the actual number that are at risk of extinction. The International Union for the Conservation of Nature took a sample of **15,674 plant species** and found that **121** were extinct and **9,390** were at threat of extinction.

The plants were placed in the following categories:

Vulnerable: high risk of endangerment in the wild

Endangered: high risk of extinction in the wild

Critically endangered: extremely high risk of extinction in the wild

Extinct in the wild: known only to survive in botanic gardens

Extinct: no known individuals remaining

Out of the **15,674 plants** assessed, just under **60%** were found to fall into the vulnerable to extinct categories. If we apply this percentage to the **321,212 species of plants** then it's possible that **192,432 plants** are at risk. That's about **three in five plant species** at risk!

RESULTS FROM SAMPLE SELECTION:

15,674 PLANT SPECIES

Vulnerable: 4,914

Endangered: 2,655

Critically endangered: 1,821

Extinct: 121

VULNERABLE
Name: Eastern Cape giant cycad
Plant category: Cycad, a species that links ferns and conifers
Habitat: coastal areas, river banks and mountain foothills of South Africa
Threats: destruction for holiday resort developments and use in traditional medicines.
Population number: estimated at **10,000** Thought to have declined by **30%** in the past **50 years**

ENDANGERED
Name: Bentgrass
Plant category: Flowering
Habitat: rocky slopes and open patches of land on islands off the South Atlantic Ocean
Threat: erosion of land and fires; introduction of alien plants in habitats preventing their growth
Population number: estimated that fewer than **250** exist in the wild

CRITICALLY ENDANGERED
Name: Amazon lily
Plant category: Flowering
Habitat: Colombian rainforests
Threat: large-scale deforestation
Population number: unknown. Not been recorded in the wild since 1853. Thought to be extinct

CRITICALLY ENDANGERED
Name: Jellyfish tree
Plant category: Flowering
Habitat: Granite slopes near the coast of islands in the Indian Ocean
Population number: Thought to be extinct in 1930 until six trees were found in 1970. Today, **50 trees** are known to exist

EXTINCT
Name: Cry pansy
Plant category: Flowering
History: Originally from France, growing in areas around limestone, its habitat was largely destroyed through quarrying. Plant population also drastically reduced as it became a popular flower for collectors. Last seen in 1927

MOST THREATENED

Amphibians

Coral

The world's plants are as threatened with extinction as mammals.

Plants and Mammals

Birds

LEAST THREATENED

LIFE FORMS AT THREAT OF EXTINCTION

THERE ARE TEN THOUSAND POISONOUS PLANTS IN THE WORLD

Plants are unable to run and hide from their predators and so have developed other means of protecting themselves. Some plants, like rose bushes or cacti, have thorns or spines to discourage animals from coming near them. Other plants have poison, which can make an animal incredibly sick or even kill them.

There are around **10,000 poisonous plant species**. They can be release their poison by touch or by eating them, some causing short-term illness, others death.

Poisonous plants have toxins that can be found in their sap, leaves or berries.

MOST POISONOUS

Many botanists consider the castor oil plant to be the most poisonous plant in the world. The castor oil plant grows in tropical conditions and produces a highly toxic seed, called the castor bean.

CASTOR BEANS

If you eat a castor bean that breaks open inside your digestive system, you may find that within:

2-3 HOURS
you experience a burning sensation in your mouth and throat, stomach pain and diarrhoea containing traces of blood;

1-3 DAYS
you experience severe dehydration and a decrease in urine;

3-5 DAYS
you die.

THE BELLADONNA PLANT can be found growing wild in Europe, North America and South-west Asia. Also known as deadly nightshade, all parts of this plant are poisonous.

Eating a single leaf will kill you.

Eating **five berries** will kill you.

1 2 3 4 5

Eating the roots will kill you.

STINGING PLANTS

STINGING NETTLES

The most common stinging plant found in Europe, North America and parts of Asia is the stinging nettle.

Nettles have hairy leaves, and hairs on their stem.

Each hair has a bulbous tip. Upon contact this tip breaks off to leave a sharp, needle-like tube that pieces the skin, injecting a toxin. This toxin can leave raised bumps on the skin and an itching sensation which can last up to **12 hours**.

GYMPIE-GYMPIE STINGING TREE

The gympie-gympie stinging tree, found in the rainforests of Australia and Indonesia, is the only stinging plant that is believed to cause death from its stings. It has been known to kill dogs and horses that have brushed up against it.

A gympie sting has been described as like being burnt with hot acid and electrocuted at the same time!

CARNIVOROUS PLANTS

All plants get their food through photosynthesis. However some plants are themselves predators and will trap and eat animals in order to get more nutrients to help them grow.

PITCHER PLANTS

There are **120 species** of pitcher plant. The giant pitcher plant is the largest of all carnivorous plants. Discovered in the Philippines, it produces a sweet smelling-nectar inside its jar-like head.

Nectar attracts insects and small mammals that fall inside.

Creatures are unable to climb out due to the sticky walls inside and end up dissolving in a pool of acid and enzymes.

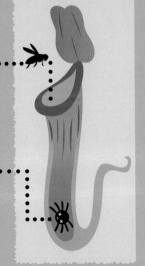

VENUS FLYTRAPS

The Venus flytrap eats small insects, enclosing them within its traps.

The trap opens at an average of **45 degrees**. 45°

20

The trap closes when an insect touches a single hair twice, or **two separate hairs** within **20 seconds** of each other.

11

OXYGEN IS RENEWED BY PLANTS EVERY TWO THOUSAND YEARS

The food we eat and the oxygen we breathe are both formed by plants through a process called photosynthesis.

PHOTOSYNTHESIS INGREDIENTS

LIGHT ENERGY + WATER H2O + CARBON DIOXIDE O C O + CHLOROPHYLL

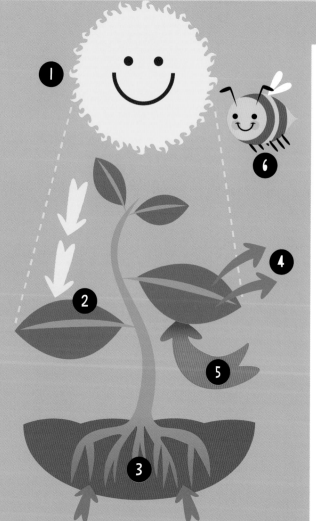

STEP 1
Light from the Sun shines down onto a plant. The plant's cells absorb this light.

STEP 2
Inside the plant cells is a substance called chlorophyll. Chlorophyll traps the Sun's light.

STEP 3
Water is absorbed into the plant through its roots underground. Water is made up of the elements hydrogen and oxygen.

STEP 4
Inside the plant, the oxygen and hydrogen from the water separates from each other; the oxygen is released into the atmosphere.

STEP 5
Carbon dioxide from the air is absorbed through the plant's leaves. The carbon dioxide combines with the hydrogen to make a form of sugar the plant can use as food.

STEP 6
Animals also use the sugar produced by the plants as food.

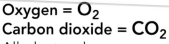

Oxygen = O_2
Carbon dioxide = CO_2
All plants release oxygen into the Earth's atmosphere.
All living creatures breathe in oxygen to keep them alive and breathe out carbon dioxide, which is absorbed by plants.

FOOD CHAINS

Plants are at the start of every food chain. All animal life depends upon plants for food.

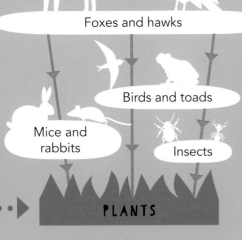

Foxes and hawks

Birds and toads

Mice and rabbits

Insects

PLANTS

CHLOROPHYLL COLOUR

Chlorophyll is the reason why most plants are green. During photosynthesis plants absorb the different colours that make up the Sun's light. However chlorophyll is not able to absorb the colour green and so it reflects it back, which is why we see green plants.

REFLECTED GREEN

LEAF

THE EARTH'S OXYGEN

Scientists believe that when the Earth was formed **4,500,000,000 years ago** the Earth's atmosphere was largely made up of carbon dioxide. The process of photosynthesis by plants meant that the proportion of oxygen increased. This increase in oxygen helped develop the variety of life that is now on Earth.

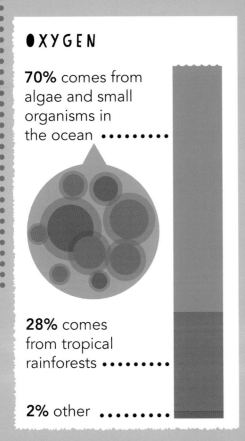

OXYGEN

70% comes from algae and small organisms in the ocean ·········

28% comes from tropical rainforests ·········

2% other ·········

OXYGEN IN THE AIR IS RENEWED BY PLANTS EVERY 2,000 YEARS.

Each carbon dioxide molecule in the atmosphere is absorbed into a plant every **200 years**.

A POMEGRANATE CAN HAVE AS MANY AS 1,370 SEEDS

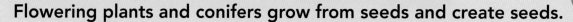

Flowering plants and conifers grow from seeds and create seeds.

Conifers have their seeds protected inside cones. A cone's scales open up to release its seeds.

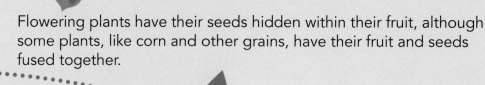

Flowering plants have their seeds hidden within their fruit, although some plants, like corn and other grains, have their fruit and seeds fused together.

One apple can produce as many as **20 seeds**.

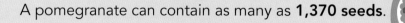

A pomegranate can contain as many as **1,370 seeds**.

Some orchids have seed pods that can hold around **3,000,000,000 seeds**.

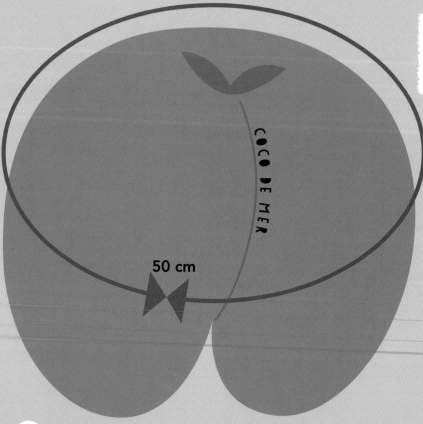

COCO DE MER

50 cm

A NUT IS A FRUIT MADE OF A HARD SHELL AND A SEED INSIDE.

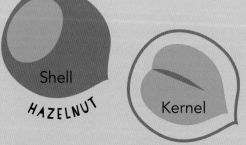

Shell

HAZELNUT

Kernel

The largest seed in the world comes from a nut from a plant called coco de mer. The hard shell has two lobes giving it the name 'the double coconut'. It can have a girth measuring up to **50 cm**, and can weigh up to **17.6 kg**.

SEED DISPERSAL

Plants disperse their seeds in different ways, so that when plants grow they don't crowd each other or have to compete for water or light.

WATER

Plants on a riverbank or seashore drop their seeds into the water, which then float away to grow further away. Some coconuts have floated **2,000 km** before finding dry land.

EXPLOSIONS

Some plants have seed pods which explode, scattering their seeds. As a pod begins to dry out it shrinks. At the same time the seeds ripen and grow bigger, and burst out of the pod.

ANIMAL

Some plants have seeds that are sticky or have small hooks that attach to animal fur. The animal then transports the seeds to a new place. Animals and birds also poo out the seeds that are in the fruit they eat.

WIND

Some fruits are so light that they and their seeds can be blown away by the wind. The seeds of the dandelion flower get dispersed by the wind.

SPORES

Mosses and ferns are non-seed plants. They produce spores. Spores are tiny reproductive cells. On ferns, they are often contained within tiny brown-black dots on the leaf. On mosses they can be found in their capsules. The spores are transported from the plants by wind or water. A single fern frond can hold up to **750,000 spores**.

The dandelion flower has bright yellow petals. When these petals die out, seeds grow on the flower head.

One dandelion flower head produces **200 seeds.**

TRAVELLING DISTANCE:

99.5 per cent of dandelion seeds travel less than **10 metres**

0.05 per cent travel more than **10 metres**

One kilometre

0.014 per cent travel more than **one kilometre**

IT CAN TAKE 312 WEEKS FROM SEED TO APPLE

When a seed starts to grow it begins a process called germination. This starts with a tiny root and shoot sprouting out through the coating of the seed.

PARTS OF A SEED

········· Shoot
········· Seed coat
········· Food store
········· Root

GERMINATION

Seed

Seedling

Leaves

Plant

Stem

WHEN DO SEEDS GROW?

Seeds can survive for a long time before they begin to grow into a plant. The time it takes for a seed to germinate depends on it receiving enough water and being in the right type of soil at the correct temperature.

Number of days for a seed to germinate according to temperature

Degrees C °	0°	5°	10°	15°	20°	25°	30°	36°
Parsnip	172	57	27	20	14	15	32	
Onion	136	50	13	7	5	4	4	13
Carrot		50	17	10	7	7	6	9
Pea		46	14	9	8	8	6	9
Tomato			43	14	14	6	6	9
Pepper			25	25	13	8	8	9
Watermelon			12		12	12	4	3

16

CAMPION

OLDEST SEED

The oldest seed to grow into a plant was dated as **32,000 years old**. It grew into a narrow-leafed campion, a flowering plant native to Siberia. It's believed to have been buried by a squirrel during the Ice Age.

RATES OF GROWTH

Once germinated, it can take an apple seed **six to ten years** to grow into a tree and bear fruit. However, it's very hard to grow an apple tree that will produce a large crop from seeds. Because of this, fruit-bearing apple trees are mainly grown from grafting, which can help them produce fruit more quickly. Grafting is a technique whereby parts of two plants are joined together. To achieve this, the stem of one plant's rootstock needs to be cut and joined to the stem of another plant.

Grafting

Rootstock

Rootstock can determine the plant's eventual size. Apple tree rootstock is sold with a tag telling the buyer how big their tree, once grafted, will grow.

THE SIZES ARE:

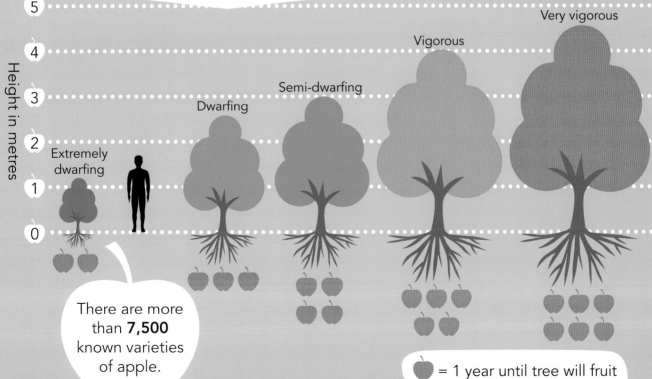

Very vigorous

Vigorous

Semi-dwarfing

Dwarfing

Height in metres

Extremely dwarfing

5

4

3

2

1

0

There are more than **7,500** known varieties of apple.

 = 1 year until tree will fruit

17

THERE ARE MORE THAN 300 TYPES OF HONEY

Honey is made from nectar that bees collect from flowers. While collecting nectar bees also collect pollen, taking part in the process of plant pollination.

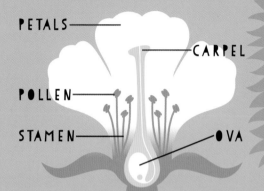

PETALS
CARPEL
POLLEN
STAMEN
OVA

Before flowers can produce fruit and seeds, they must be pollinated. This happens when the pollen from a flower joins to an ova hidden inside a flower.

Flowers contain stamens, at the top of which is the pollen. Flowers also have a carpel which holds an ova that the pollen needs to reach in order to allow the plant to grow its seeds and fruit.

POLLINATORS

Pollination is enabled by pollinators. They take the pollen from one flower to another. Pollinators include the wind, waves, human activity and animals such as:

BEES   BUTTERFLIES   BEETLES   ANTS   FLIES   BATS   HUMMINGBIRDS

An estimated one out of every three bites of food comes to us through the work of animal pollinators.

ANIMAL POLLINATION

Many insects and birds feed off flowers. They are attracted to them by their bright colours and sweet smells.

Pollen is sticky and attaches itself to the creatures that have been drawn to the flower.

When the creature then visits another of these flowers, the pollen gets rubbed from its body onto the top of the carpel.

Once the pollen has attached itself to the carpel, it travels down to join the ova. The plant has now been pollinated as the pollen and ova join together to make seeds.

Some flowers are pollinated by the wind. Their pollen is carried through the air.

HAY FEVER

Pollen contains proteins that can cause an allergic reaction in some people. This is known as hay fever.

Symptoms:

RUNNY NOSE

ITCHY EYES

SNEEZING

FLOWER POLLEN

Causes:

TREE POLLEN

GRASS POLLEN

BEES

It takes a colony of around **74,132 bees** to pollinate one hectare of fruit trees.

ONE HECTARE

A worker bee gathers enough honey to make **1/10 teaspoon of honey** in their entire life.

While collecting the pollen, bees feed off the nectar from flowers, which they carry back to their hives to make honey.

There are more than **300 different types of honey**, each type made from the nectar of a different flower.

19

Trees are the tallest free-standing living things in the world. They also live longer than any other organism on Earth.

The oldest tree is a jurupa oak tree, in California, USA. It is said to be **13,000 years old**, making it the oldest living organism.
The oldest person to have lived reached the age of **122 years old**.
If the life of the oldest tree were measured as being **24 hours**, then the oldest person would have been alive for **14 minutes and 30 seconds** of that time.

12 hours

12 hours

14 minutes and 30 seconds

Lifespan of oldest person

Lifespan of oldest tree

The tree with the broadest trunk is a Montezuma cypress, in Oaxaca, Mexico. The trunk's diameter is **14 metres**, with a girth of **42 metres**.

The tallest living tree is a coast redwood, growing in the Redwood National Park, California, USA. It measures **115.55 metres** high.

The smallest tree is the dwarf willow tree. It rarely grows above **five centimetres**.

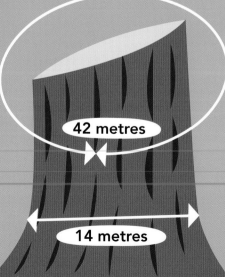
42 metres

14 metres

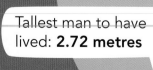
Tallest man to have lived: **2.72 metres**

TREE, SHRUB OR HERBACEOUS PLANT?

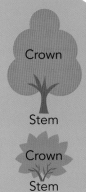

Crown

Stem

Crown

Stem

The difference between trees and shrubs is in the growth form of the stem. Trees have a single woody stem from which branches grow to form a crown. Shrubs have multiple woody stems which arise at ground level forming a crown at a lower level.

A herbaceous plant is a plant that does not have much wood and its stems are green and soft. You may hear people say that bananas grow on banana trees, but the banana actually grows on a herbaceous plant known as musa.

DECIDUOUS TREES

SUMMER   WINTER

Deciduous plants are those that lose all of their leaves for part of the year. Depending on the region, this usually coincides with winter, or the dry season. The leafless trees need less water. Before the tree sheds its leaves, the leaf colour may change, as less green chlorophyll is made and other colours show through.

An oak tree sheds around 250,000 leaves a year.

EVERGREEN TREES

An evergreen tree has leaves all year round and these leaves remain green. Most trees that have needles for leaves are evergreen. These leaves have been adapted to slow down the loss of water vapour, allowing them to survive in cold and dry seasons. They have a wax-like waterproof coating.

TREES HAVE LEAVES OF MANY DIFFERENT SHAPES AND SIZES

Simple

Doubly-serrate

Compound or lobed

Star-shaped

Heart-shaped or cordate

Lanceolate

Linear

Deltoid

100 SPECIES OF MOSS GROW IN THE ANTARCTIC

Few plants are able to grow in very dry or cold places, or where there isn't much sunlight.

Out of the **16,236 species of moss** in the world, only **100** grow in the Antarctic. **Six different species** of moss grow on the islands of East Antarctica. The mosses that survive here have an unusual food source. In addition to the sunlight they get from photosynthesis, they get extra nutrients from penguin poo left behind **thousands of years ago**.

—1 year
—2 years
—3 years

The mosses on the islands of East Antarctica grow just **three millimetres** a year.

BIOMES

The Earth is often divided up into different biomes. These are places that have specific temperatures and landscape that allow certain plants to grow there.

Equator

BIOMES:

- **Tundra:** treeless, cold climate
- **Taiga:** forested areas with wet summers and long cold winters
- **Grasslands:** vast grassy terrain with hot summers and cold winters
- **Desert:** dry and hot with little plant growth
- **Tropical rainforest:** hot and wet densely forested regions
- **Temperate rainforest:** cool and wet forested regions
- **Polar:** very cold with permanent presence of ice and snow

ANTARCTICA ①

Coldest place on Earth
Average temperature: -57°C
Coldest recorded temperature: -89.2°C
The majority of the Antarctic continent is covered by permanent ice and snow leaving less than **1% of land** suitable for plants to grow. Due to the cold, harsh conditions on the Antarctic, no trees are able to grow there, but some mosses have adapted to the harsh conditions.

ATACAMA DESERT, CHILE ❷

Driest place on Earth
Average temperature: 22°C

A cactus can grow in hot, dry places like deserts. Its roots are near the top of the ground so that it can take in water quickly when it rains. It stores water in its stem.

Only **three cacti** are native to this region. As it rains very little here, these cacti get the majority of their water from the ocean fog that blows over the desert.

DASHT-E LUT, IRAN ❸

Hottest place on Earth
Highest recorded temperature: 70°C
No plants or creatures are recorded as living here.

SAHARA DESERT, AFRICA ❹

Average temperature: 30°C
Some plants in the Sahara Desert have extensive root systems that can go deep into the ground to get water. The roots of the welwitschia mirabilis go as deep as **50 metres**.

AMAZON RAINFOREST, BRAZIL ❺

Average temperature: 27°C
The Amazon rainforest has a tropical climate, providing a constant supply of water and sunlight for broad-leafed plants.

40,000 different plant species can be found here. This is the largest variety of plant species to be found in one area.

SVALBARD, NORWAY ❻

Average temperature: 4°C
Only **165 species of plant** have been found to survive the tundra of Svalbard.

The Arctic buttercup lives here and is able to survive by living in groups close to the ground, sheltering them from the strong cold winds.

UNDERWATER

Seagrasses, found near the coastal waters of most continents, are the only plants that can produce flowers underwater. They are pollinated by the waves, which carry their pollen.

80-85 COCOA BEANS IN AN AVERAGE CHOCOLATE BAR

Plants provide a main source of food for all living creatures.
Humans eat fruit and vegetables raw or cooked and also as an ingredient in other foods, such as chocolate or bread.

THE WORLD'S LARGEST CUCUMBER MEASURED 1.1 METRES.

Fruit grows from the flower of a plant, but vegetables come from different parts of different plants.

 ROOTS: CARROTS

 **STEM: ASPARAGUS**

 **LEAVES: CABBAGES**

 FLOWER: BROCCOLI

DIETS

Many animals just eat plants; they are called herbivores. Humans who choose to eat only plants are called vegans.

It's important to have a balanced diet. This means eating a variety of foods, ensuring that you receive the right nutrients that your body needs to stay healthy. Some nutrients are easily found in meat and dairy products, but if you are a vegan it's important that you eat the right foods to supplement this.

WHAT YOUR BODY NEEDS:	PROTEIN	CALCIUM	IRON	VITAMINS
Examples of food it can be found in:	Potatoes Beans and pulses	Broccoli Almonds Kale Dried apricots	Swiss chard Chickpeas Lentils Kidney bean	Carrots Oranges Bananas Spinach

BEANS AND PULSES

Beans and pulses are edible seeds from plants. They are often contained within protective pods and include lentils, black beans, chickpeas, broad beans and kidney beans.
Lentils have been found in the tombs of ancient Egyptians, dating back to **2400 BCE**.

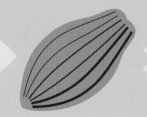

COCOA BEANS COME FROM COCOA PODS WHICH COME FROM THE CACAO TREE.

Over **3,500,000 tonnes of cocoa beans** are produced annually to be transformed into products that contain cocoa. **80–85 cocoa beans** go into an average chocolate bar.

The cacao tree is an evergreen, found in over **50 tropical countries**. It grows best when **15 degrees** north or south of the equator.

Cocoa beans are farmed in the following countries:

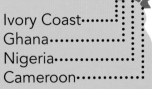

Ecuador
Brazil

Ivory Coast
Ghana
Nigeria
Cameroon

Indonesia
Kenya
Tanzania

FROM CACAO TREE TO CHOCOLATE BAR

It takes **two to three years** after the cacao tree has been planted before it produces cocoa pods, its fruit.

Every year, cacao trees grow thousands of flowers. Only around **5%** of the flowers will produce a pod.

It takes around **five months** for each pod to ripen. Once they have been cut down, the beans are then removed from their pods. There are between **30–40 beans** inside a pod.

Next, the beans are dried, often in the sun. People rake them to help the moisture escape. This takes about **one week**.

The beans are fermented to bring out the flavour and prevent them from sprouting. This is done by wrapping heaps of beans in leaf parcels or placing layers of beans in wooden crates.

The dried beans are taken to a processing plant where they are cleaned and roasted.

The beans pass through rollers. This leaves chocolate liquor, cocoa powder and cocoa butter.

The chocolate liquor is blended with some cocoa butter and other ingredients, such as sugar and milk. It is mixed for hours and then poured into chocolate bar molds.

The individuals bars are wrapped and delivered across the world for people to eat.

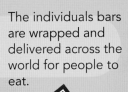

25

IT TAKES 14 TREES TO MAKE ONE TONNE OF MAGAZINE PAPER

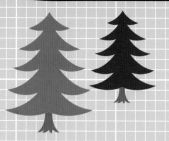

Plants not only provide you with food but feature in items all around you, such as clothes and furniture.

Paper and card are used as packaging for almost everything. Around **42%** of logging that takes place each year is for the production of paper.

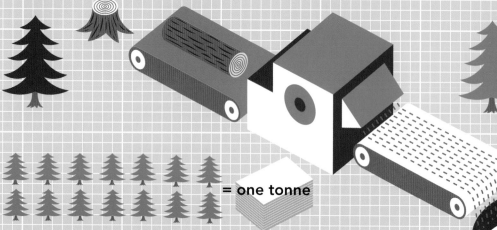

= one tonne

It takes **14 trees** to make **one tonne** of magazine paper. An average magazine weighs around **350 grams**. There are **1,000,000 grams** in **one tonne**. We can divide this weight into the weight measurement of an average magazine to work out how many magazines can be produced by one tonne of paper.

The weight of one magazine divided into one tonne = **2,857 magazines**.
It takes **14 trees** to make **2,857 magazines**.
It takes one tree to make **204 magazines**. · = 204

COTTON

The majority of clothes worn in the world are made from cotton.

Cotton grows as a soft fluffy ball that protects the seeds on cotton plants. Around **25 million tonnes of cotton** are grown each year.

Cotton was first used for clothing over **7,000 years ago**, in the Indus Valley, which is now part of India and Pakistan.

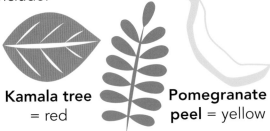

Plants are also used for dyeing clothes. This started over **5,000 years ago.** Plants that have been used for dye include:

Kamala tree = red

Pomegranate peel = yellow

Indigo fera plant = blue

MEDICINES

For hundreds of years plants have been used as medicines. Today, many extracts from plants are still used within medicines. **25%** of all medicines have been developed from tropical rainforest plants.

FOSSIL FUELS

Coal, gas and oil are known as fossil fuels. They are formed from plants and small animals that died and rotted during **millions of years**, covered by many layers of dirt deep within the ground. We use coal, gas and oil as fuel. We burn these to keep us warm and to power cars and electricity. Oil is also used to make plastics.

OCEAN 300-400,000,000 YEARS AGO

Plants and animals died and were buried under layers of sand.

OCEAN 50-100,000,000 YEARS AGO

Sand and silt

Plant and animal remains

Over millions of years these remains were buried deeper, with heat and pressure turning them into fossil fuels, such as oil and gas.

TODAY

Sand and silt rock

Oil and gas

We drill down through layers of sand and rock to reach the fossil fuels.

PLANT	USED FOR
Foxglove	Heart medication
Eucalyptus tree	Cough medicine
Quinine tree	Malaria prevention
Opium poppy	Pain reliever
Curare tree	Muscle relaxant

THE QUEEN OF THE NIGHT BLOOMS FOR ONE NIGHT EVERY YEAR

Amongst the huge number of plant life there exist some unusual plants that can amaze and disgust.

CORPSE FLOWERS

DISGUSTING PLANTS

The titan arum, found in Indonesia, is one of the world's smelliest plants. It produces flowers about every six years and when this happens, it smells like rotten meat. Because of this, it is also known as the 'corpse flower'. The flowering structure can reach up to **three metres** in height. It is surrounded by a single leaf which can grow to **six metres** tall and **five metres** wide.

RAFFLESIA ARNOLDII

1 metre

1.70 metres is the height of an average adult human being.

TITAN ARUM

Height in metres

3

3.5

2

2.5

2

1.5

1

0

The rafflesia arnoldii, from Indonesia, is also sometimes called a 'corpse flower' as it too smells of rotting meat. It has the largest flower of any plant in the world. Its flower has a diameter of around **one metre**. The rafflesia lives as a parasite on other plants.

PARASITIC PLANTS

Plants that attach themselves to other plants, and suck out nutrients from them, are known as parasitic plants. These plants manage to insert roots into their host plant.

Mistletoe is a parasitic plant. Its seeds land on their host plant in bird poo. They can grow large and bushy, to the point where it can be hard to spot the host plant's leaves amongst those of the mistletoe.

MISTLETOE ON AN APPLE TREE

GIANT WATER LILY

LARGE LEAVES

The giant water lily has a large circular leaf, also known as a lily pad, that can grow to over **2.5 metres** in diameter. The leaf can support **45 kilograms** of weight, provided it is evenly distributed over the leaf's surface.

FOR ONE NIGHT ONLY

The night-blooming cereus, also known as the 'queen of the night', is the name of a group of cacti that flower at night. Some of these only flower once a year. They grow in the deserts of Texas, the USA and north Mexico. The flowers are trumpet-shaped, up to **10 centimetres** wide and **20 centimetres** long.

NIGHT-BLOOMING CEREUS

FURTHER INFORMATION

BOOKS

Project Science: Plants by Sally Hewitt (Franklin Watts, 2012)
Science F.A.Q.: Do Plants Really Eat Insects? by Thomas Canavan (Franklin Watts, 2014)
Super Science: Flowering Plants by Rob Colson (Franklin Watts, 2010)
The World in Infographics: The Natural World by Jon Richards and Ed Simkins (Wayland, 2012)

WEBSITES

Games and information on how to grow plants and information on the environmental issues surrounding tropical rainforests:
www.sciencekids.co.nz/plants.html
Activity with instructions on how to grow your own miniature garden:
kids.nationalgeographic.com/kids/activities/crafts/miniature-garden/
Information on the importance of trees with links to games:
www.ecokids.ca/pub/eco_info/topics/climate/tree_planting/why_plant_trees.cfm

Note to parents and teachers:

Every effort has been made by the publisher to ensure that these websites contain no inappropriate or offensive material. However, because of the nature of the Internet, it is impossible to guarantee that the content of these sites will not be altered. We strongly advise that Internet access is supervised by a responsible adult.

LARGE NUMBERS

1,000,000,000,000,000,000,000,000,000,000,000 = ONE DECILLION
1,000,000,000,000,000,000,000,000,000,000 = ONE NONILLION
1,000,000,000,000,000,000,000,000,000 = ONE OCTILLION
1,000,000,000,000,000,000,000,000 = ONE SEPTILLION
1,000,000,000,000,000,000,000 = ONE SEXTILLION
1,000,000,000,000,000,000 = ONE QUINTILLION
1,000,000,000,000,000 = ONE QUADRILLION
1,000,000,000,000 = ONE TRILLION
1,000,000,000 = ONE BILLION
1,000,000 = ONE MILLION
1000 = ONE THOUSAND
100 = ONE HUNDRED
10 = TEN
1 = ONE

GLOSSARY

algae	a simple form of plant often found in water. Some seaweeds are algae
allergic reaction	when your body reacts to a particular substance, causing iritation, such as itchy eyes or a rash
biomes	large areas on Earth that are defined by their plant life and climate
botany	the scientific study of plants
carbon dioxide	a gas that humans breathe out and plants absorb
carnivorous	the description of an organism that eats animals
chlorophyll	a green pigment found in plants that helps them absorb light and produce their food
conifers	trees and shrubs that have cones, and are mostly evergreen
deciduous	trees that shed their leaves during a season of the year
dehydration	when something is dry, after water loss
endangered	at risk of extinction
estimate	an approximate calculation
evergreen	a plant that has leaves which remain green all year round
evolved	when something has developed over a long period of time
extinct	having no living members; a species that has died out
fossil fuel	fuel made up of the remains of organisms that have been compressed underground
frond	a large leaf, like those on a fern, that splits into different sections
germination	the process whereby something begins to grow and develop, such as a seedling sprouting out from a seed
grafting	attaching one part of a plant to another plant to grow together
habitat	the environment or home of a creature or plant
herbivore	the description of an organism that only eats plants
invasive species	organisms that invade and modify an environment of which they are not naturally a part
liverwort	small green non-flowering plant, similar to moss but with a more distinctive leaf structure
moss	green, dense, non-flowering plant that grows in damp areas
nectar	a sugary substance produced by plants and made into honey by bees
nutrients	a substance that is beneficial to growth and well-being
organism	a living thing
oxygen	a gas that plants produce and humans breathe in to live
parasite	an organism that lives off another organism
photosynthesis	the process by which plants create their own food and produce oxygen
pollen	dust-like grains on a flower that are required to be carried to another plant for fertilisation
pollination	the process whereby pollen is transferred from one plant to another
rhizome	an underground root-like structure that bears shoots
sap	a fluid that circulates around a plant, carrying nutrients and water
species	living things that contain shared characteristics, e.g. human beings
spores	the reproductive cells of ferns and mosses
stamen	the fertilising organ of a plant
toxic	a poisonous substance

INDEX

algae 4, 6, 7, 13
Amazon 23
Amazon lilies 9
Antarctica 22, 23
apples/apple trees 14, 16–17, 29
Arctic buttercups 23
Atacama Desert 23
atmosphere, Earth's 12–13

bananas 21, 24
bees 18–19
belladonna plants 10
bentgrass 9
biomes 22–23
botanists 5, 8, 10
botany 5

cacti 10, 23, 29
campions 17
carbon dioxide 4, 12–13
carpel 18
castor oil plants 10
chains, food 13
chocolate 24, 25
chlorophyll 12–13, 21
coal 27
coco de mer 14
cocoa 24, 25
coconuts 14, 15
conifers 4, 6, 7, 9, 14
cotton 27
counting plants 5
cry pansies 9

dandelions 15
Dasht-e Lut 23
deadly nightshades 10
deserts 6, 23, 29
diatoms 7
diet, balanced 24
dwarf willow trees 20
dyes 27

Eastern Cape giant cycads 9

ferns 4, 6, 7, 9, 15
flowers 6, 7, 15, 18, 19, 21, 24, 25, 28, 29
    parts of a flower 18
food 4, 12–13, 24–15, 26
fruit 14, 15, 16, 17, 18, 19, 24, 25

fuels, fossil 27
fungi 7

gas 27
giant water lilies 29
grafting 17
gympie-gympie stinging trees 11

hay fever 19
honey 18–19

International Union for the Conservation of Nature 8

jellyfish trees 9
jurupa oak trees 20

leaves 4, 6, 7, 10, 11, 12, 13, 15, 16, 21, 24, 28, 29
liverworts 4, 6
logging 8, 26

medicines 4, 9, 27
mistletoe 29
Montezuma cypress 20
mosses 4, 6, 7, 15, 22–23

nectar 11, 18, 19
night-blooming cereus 29
nuts 14

oceans 6, 7, 13, 23, 27
oil 27
orchids 14
ova 18
oxygen 4, 12–13

paper 26
penguins 22
photosynthesis 4, 11, 12–13, 22
pitcher plants 11
plants
    carnivorous 11
    counting 6–7
    endangered 8–9
    extinct 8–9
    flowering 4, 6, 7, 9, 14, 15, 17
    herbaceous 21

    medicinal 27
    parasitic 28, 29
    parts of a plant 6, 18
    poisonous 10–11
    pollination 18–19, 23
    smelliest 28
    vulnerable 8–9
pollen 18, 19, 23
pollinators 18–19
pomegranates 14, 27

'queen of the night' 28, 29

rafflesia arnoldii 28
rainforests 5, 6, 9, 11, 13, 23, 27
redwoods 20
roots 4, 6, 7, 10, 12, 16, 17, 23, 24, 29
rootstock 17

Sahara Desert 23
seagrass 23
seaweed 6, 7
seeds 7, 10, 14–17, 18, 24, 27, 29
    dispersal 15
    germination 16, 17
shrubs 21
spores 15
stamen 18
stinging nettles 11
Svalbard 34

titan arums 28
toxins, plant 10, 11
trees 5, 6, 9, 11, 17, 20–21, 22, 23, 24–26
    apple 18–19
    cocoa 24–25
    dating rings 5
    deciduous 21
    evergreen 21, 25
    leaf shapes 21
    oldest 20

Venus flytraps 11

welwitschia mirabilis 23
World Conservation Unit 6

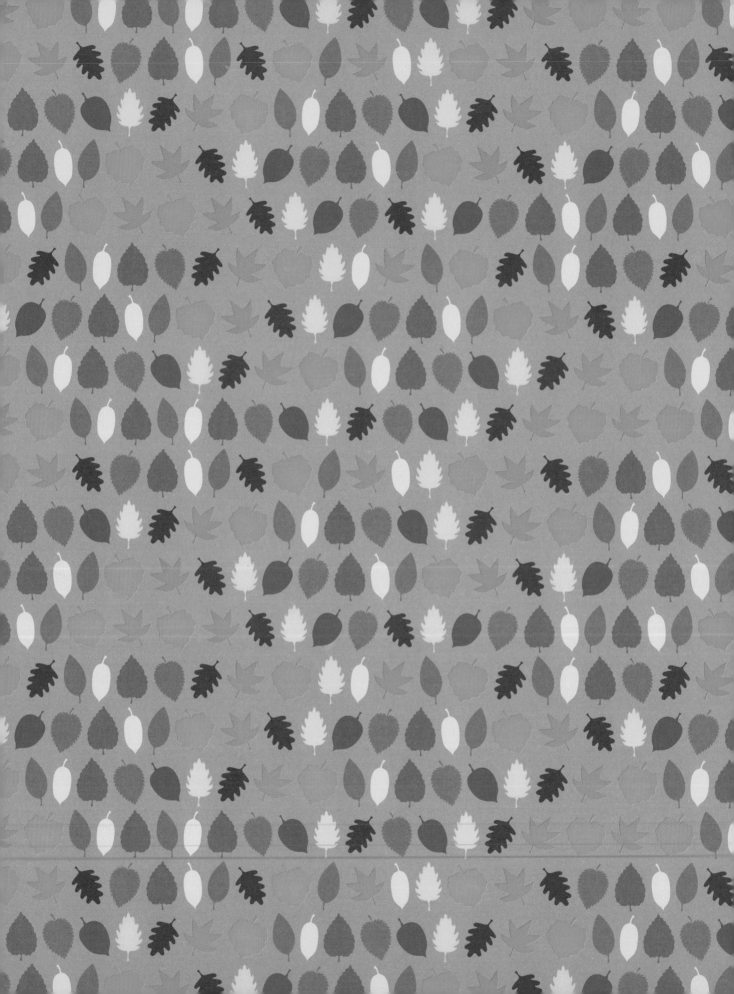